Writing Picture Books

What works and what doesn't!

Kathy Stinson

Pembroke Publishers Limited

Pembroke Publishers Limited
538 Hood Road
Markham, Ontario
L3R 3K9

Canadian Cataloguing in Publication Data

Stinson, Kathy
   Writing picture books

Includes bibliographical references.
ISBN 0-921217-72-2

1. Picture-books for children — Authorship.
I. Title.

PN147.5.S75 1991   808.06′8   C91-095047-4

Editor: David Kilgour
Design: John Zehethofer
Illustrations: Sharon Matthews
Typesetting: Jay Tee Graphics Ltd.

Printed and bound in Canada
9 8 7 6 5 4 3 2

Contents

Introduction

Many books have been written with the objective of helping writers write better books, but few have been written to help writers write better picture book stories. There may be several reasons why this is so:

- Writing a picture book story is too easy for anyone to need help doing it.

- What makes a picture book work is its pictures.

- What makes a picture book text successful is too elusive to grasp.

Of course, writing a picture book is *not* too easy for anyone to need help doing it. Anyone who has tried their hand at writing a picture book and, with a vague sense of dissatisfaction with the result, has relegated it to the bottom of a drawer knows that writing a picture book is not easy. Anyone who, with confidence and high hopes, has sent a picture book manuscript to a publisher, only to see it returned with a form letter saying basically, "Thanks, but no thanks", knows it too. Anyone with a collection of such manuscripts and rejection letters certainly knows that writing a picture book is not easy.

Of course, writing any book is not easy. But there are factors unique to picture book stories that make writing them particularly difficult. Not more difficult than writing a novel necessarily, or writing non-fiction, but difficult in its own way, and certainly more difficult than most people would expect, considering the brevity and apparent simplicity of most picture books.

A picture book story is often read aloud by an adult to a child. Many times. So it must appeal to both an adult audience and a child audience. It must stand up to repeated readings. If it is to be read by a child alone, that child has probably only recently mastered the ability to read. All of these factors must be considered in the writing of a picture book manuscript.

And what makes a picture book successful is *not* its pictures alone. Quality illustration is, of course, essential to the success of a picture book. But even the best illustration cannot bring to life a poorly written text. The most successful picture books are those in which good text and good illustration complement each other in a comfortable balance.

What makes a successful picture book text *may* be extremely difficult to grasp. There is a subjective element in how a person responds to a picture book, as there is with any book. A book that "works" for a particular reader may seem to have a certain magic, for that reader. No one can tell a writer how to put magic into a book. It has as much to do with what's in the reader as what's in the book. And that the writer has no control over.

But there are aspects of picture book stories that can be addressed, pitfalls that writers can avoid, tips that can assist them in evaluating and improving texts they may already have written or will write in the future.

My ideas about writing are, of course, rooted in my own experiences as a writer. You may want to adapt them for your own needs, your own audience. Whether you are a parent writing stories for your own children, a teacher writing for the children in your classes, or a writer anticipating publication of your picture book(s), this book has been written for you.

Kathy Stinson
Toronto, June 1991

CHAPTER ONE

So you want to write a picture book?

Have you read any good picture books lately?

Most writing teachers, most books on the subject of writing, will emphasize the fact that one learns to write well by writing. So write every day, certainly, take a writing course if you wish, attend writing conferences if you are able.

But above all, before you sit down to write — read. There is probably no other single thing that you can do to help you learn to write well than reading good writing in the area in which you are interested. Picture books of all kinds, and poetry, folktales, or fantasy, too, if your interests are more specific.

In reading well-written picture books, you will discover the tremendous range of picture book subject matter, you will see how other writers handle language, drawing their readers into their books, bringing their stories to satisfying conclusions. If you have no specific interests, you might discover the kind of book you are most interested in writing. Or you might discover that writing picture books is not for you. If you don't enjoy reading picture books, it is unlikely that you will be able to write one that "works".

To illustrate points about various aspects of picture books in the upcoming chapters of this book, I will refer to many picture books that "work" for me. If none of the references mean anything to you, you may not be ready yet to write a picture book, never mind offer it to your children or submit it to a publisher. You must be familiar with the best already available, if you are to judge the quality of work you are doing yourself.

However, the picture books I mention will be my own personal favourites. If they don't sound familiar to you, but you find yourself wondering why I didn't mention this book or that one, particular favourites of your own, then you may well be ready to sit down to write your book, or present what you have written to your intended readers or potential publisher. (A full list of recommended books appears in the bibliography at the end of this book.)

Adult novelists don't write until they have read a lot of adult novels. Writers of books for children owe their audiences the same training.

"But what if I'm influenced by what I read? Won't I just sound like everyone else if I read what other people have written?"

Don't worry about being "influenced" by the fine writing you will read. You have been influenced, whether you have been aware of it or not, by everything you have read since you began reading, and if you are like most people you've read, along with some gems, some pretty mediocre stuff. So why not expose yourself to the best writing you can find? It can only help you to find the story in you that is uniquely yours, and to find the voice in you that will tell your story most effectively.

"What should I write about? Where do I get ideas?"

Write what you know, write a book you would be interested in reading. It sounds clichéd, but there really is no other answer. Ideas are all around you, in the events of your everyday life, in the anecdotes and stories others relate to you, and in the images that pop unbidden into your head.

Like the image in author-illustrator Phoebe Gilman's mind of a tree sprouting balloons, which wouldn't leave her alone until she wrote *The Balloon Tree* a good twelve years after the image first came to her. Like *The Name of the Tree*, which Celia Lottridge remembered hearing as a child. Like the owling expeditions enjoyed by Jane Yolen's family on winter nights, which led to *Owl Moon*.

The ideas are there. Open yourself up to them and open yourself up to the young child buried deeply or not so deeply inside you, and your question will quickly change from "Where do I get ideas to write about?" to "When am I ever going to find the time to write all the neat stories I'd like to write?" It's not always easy, but writers write, no matter how hectic their lives are. You will too, when your story insists on being written.

"Once I've written my book, then what?"

Rewrite it. Odds are a kazillion to one against your story springing from your pen or word processor (no matter how many bytes it has or how much you spent on it), just right the first time.

It may never be perfect, but chapters 2 to 7 of this book will help you to evaluate what you have written, and to figure out what rewriting needs to be done to bring it a little closer to being what you hoped for, what your readers deserve.

You might ask yourself the questions posed in these chapters each time you finish a draft, until you are completely satisfied that you have written the best book you can, remembering of course the subjective elements of any book that works, the ones that no "checklist" can help you evaluate.

But before you go on there is one question you must ask yourself.

Are you interested in writing a picture book because you have a lesson to teach young children or an important message to impart to them?

A child does not go to a book looking for more of the wise lessons the adults in his or her life are always ready to impart. "Share your toys." "Eat your spinach." "Answer when you're spoken to." And most writers of books that children love know this.

There is one book, for example, in which a child insists, among many things, on wearing her red mitts even though her mother points out that her red mitts have holes in them and her brown mitts would keep her hands warmer. Obviously this disobedient child should have got frost bite. But Kathy Stinson missed her opportunity, again and again throughout *Red Is Best*, to illustrate to the child and all who read about her the dangers of disobeying Mom.

It is not that I, or any of the thousands of adults who have shared this book with children, want to encourage disobedience in young readers. But children are not going to disobey their parents as a result of reading about someone else who did, any more than they are about to stop disobeying their parents as a result of reading about someone who suffered as a result of disobeying theirs.

Children come to a book looking for a good story, and that means characters they can care about, whose antics or difficulties they can enjoy and share. They are not looking for a moral lesson, any more than you are when you pick up a book. If the story you are planning to write interests you, the writer, less than the lesson you hope to teach through it, chances are your story will not much interest your intended readers either.

CHAPTER TWO

What makes a text a picture book text?

was with big spots on and he the spots changed colour. green yellow his back when jumped...

Should the story you have written be a picture book or something else? A work of non-fiction, maybe? Or a novel?

Whether or not what you have written should be a picture book or a work of non-fiction may depend on whether or not you have a story to tell. Sometimes people think they're telling a story, but what they are really doing is trying to provide some information to children about a particular subject, like insects, or nutritious snacks. So they invent a character who is interested in that subject and away they go. What they end up with is a dialogue loosely disguised as a story in which a child character asks questions and an adult character answers them.

But most children are not interested in reading a bunch of questions and answers. *Not if they were expecting a story.* If you have a subject you're interested in that you're convinced lots of kids would be interested in too, by all means write a book about it. As a work of non-fiction.

Sometimes the temptation to bury lots of good information in a story arises out of a writer's fear that non-fiction books are dry and dull, that kids won't read them. If you share that attitude towards non-fiction, even a little bit, look at the non-fiction currently being published. Some of it is downright amazing. One publisher comes right out and says so, in a series of books, including *The Amazing Apple Book* by Paulette Bourgeois and *The Amazing Egg Book* by Margaret Griffin and Deborah Seed. You will probably find yourself saying, as another popular non-fiction book is titled, "I didn't know that," about non-fiction books and about the material in them. Once you see the exciting possibilities for presenting information to kids, you may see what you thought was your picture book "story" in a whole new way.

If you have written a story in which there is a lot of text but not much complication in terms of plot or character development, you may need to make a decision as to which direction you would prefer to take. For a younger picture book audience you will want to reduce the amount of text. Sometimes eliminating parts of the text that will be explained by the book's visuals goes a long way towards reducing the text to a more manageable length. For an older "chapter book" audience, you will want to introduce more complexity into the story. You may need more characters, a twist in plot, or more development of the characters and ideas.

Ted Staunton's handling of character and plot, first in a picture book called *Taking Care of Crumley*, and then in a collection of stories about the same characters for older children, called *Maggie and Me*, shows the kinds of books these options might lead to. In the picture book story, the characters are developed only as far as they need be to tell the story of how Maggie gets Ugly Augie and his Goons to leave Cyril alone. In *Maggie and Me* the characters are older and more complex, but consistent with their development in the picture book. The stories in both books are told in the first person from Cyril's point of view, but the stories for older kids are longer and involve somewhat more complex situations.

Can you imagine your text illustrated in an interesting way?

What you have written will never be a picture book if it cannot be illustrated in an interesting way, within the confines of the structure of a picture book. An artist with a more visual sense than you have will likely be hired to illustrate your book, if it is to be published, bringing possibilities to it you never imagined. But there are some things even a non-visually-oriented person can check on.

Read your text, imagining it as a book. Divide the text according to possible page divisions, keeping in mind that a standard length for a picture book is thirty-two pages, including the title page(s) and copyright page. Consider whether the text allows room for illustrations, and, whether your intention is publication or not, room for a variety of scenes, moods, and activities in the illustrations as you move from page to page. Movement and change within the text will enable an artist to create illustrations with energy and vitality.

If you find yourself thinking that your story will be really good once it's illustrated, think again. While a picture book story is certainly enhanced by good illustration, indeed made accessible to its young readership that way, the text itself must be excellent — on its own — before any thought is given to illustration. A weakly written story leaning on excellent illustration will enjoy only limited success, none of it attributable to your efforts. Besides, and more importantly, a picture book that is only half well-done is cheating its readers, and why would you want any part in that?

CHAPTER THREE

Language and style

Because you have written a book for very young readers, have you taken special care with your language?

Care must be taken with language, no matter who your audience is.

Now, when you write your little book for children, be sure that all the wordsies have a natural flow. Do you know what that means? It means that they go together well. And although you're writing for cutiekins, remember that they can handle real words, and even big ones too. Hardly any of them need to be coated with sugar. Sugar rots stories just as surely as it rots little toofies. Did you know that young readers don't appreciate language or an approach that is demeaning? Demeaning. That's a big word, isn't it? Publishers sometimes make little pukies when they have to read stories that fail to respect children's dignity.

This is an obvious and gross exaggeration to illustrate a point that must not be missed. Your style must respect the intelligence and dignity of your readers. Writing that seriously violates this requirement has often been written by someone who has not given adequate consideration to their motivation to write for young children. "Cute" stories are often trite, and reflect a poor understanding of a toddler's world. It is possible that a writer having difficulty overcoming cuteness in style or in content is too out of touch with the child's world to be trying to write for that age group. If the idea that a toddler has either intelligence or dignity surprises or amuses you, then you might be one of those people.

Watch for the word "little". Its use as an adjective to describe something small is often legitimate, but it can have a trivializing impact on what you are writing about, especially if it is used often. If you're not sure what I mean by this, consider how you feel when someone asks you how the little book you're working on is coming along.

You may be able to detect other problems in the area of language by reading your story out loud to yourself so that you can hear the words. If they sound stiff, perhaps you are using words that are old-fashioned in a story that does not call for old-fashioned language, or words that are simply not you. You might try telling your story aloud before writing it down, if you are one of those people who seem to slip into using overly formal language when they begin to write.

Of course some stories, no matter how recently written, call for a formal style of language — for example, Michael Bedard's *The Lightning Bolt*, reminiscent in style of many classic folktales.

Be sure that your characters sound like who they are. Is a child told to put on a much hated snowsuit likely to say, "Mother, I would prefer not to do that," or *"Nnnnno!"*? Errors are rarely as glaring as this, but even a small slip out of character can seriously affect the believablity of your whole story.

Language can be simple and rich at the same time. It can't be tacked on to make a story sound good. It flows naturally through a story that is told with respect for its reader. Look at the language in Jane Yolen's *Owl Moon*, for example, in Monica Hughes's *Little Fingerling*, or in Margaret Mahy's *The Man Whose Mother Was a Pirate* and *The Witch in the Cherry Tree*. (Margaret Mahy is a master at taking things written about time and time again in picture books — like the sea and witches — and creating wonderfully original images of them with her words.)

Do words that might be unfamiliar to your readers fit smoothly with the rest of the text?

Don't pause during narration to define unfamiliar words. Compare the effect of:

In her hand she held a 3-pronged spear which is called a trident. It too was of bright gold.

and

In her right hand she held a trident. The 3-pronged spear was bright gold like her buttons.

The meaning of trident is clear to readers in both samples of text but the words flow more easily in the second case. Also, the writer does not risk insulting those readers who already know the word's meaning when the definition is embedded naturally in the text.

Part of the reason a phrase like "which is called a . . ." is jarring to the reader has to do with the problem of authors intruding where they don't belong.

A reader comes to a book in anticipation of an intimate relationship with a story. If you yourself are not a character in the story, but you occasionally put yourself there by talking to the readers in the middle of the story, by saying such things as "which is called a hula hoop", or "This is what she saw", your comments may be felt by the reader as an intrusion into the private relationship between reader and story, because suddenly the reader is reminded of the presence of the writer. It's almost as if you're butting in. You, the writer, do not need to say, "This is what she saw." You need only to show the reader what your character did in fact see.

Have you used as few words as you need to tell your story well?

Large blocks of type can be visually intimidating to readers of picture books, whether the reader is a parent anticipating trying to hold a toddler's attention, or a youngster who has begun to master reading books independently. In either case "too many words" can slow down the movement of a story, boring a reader who might be rivetted if it weren't for those "extra" words. Be ruthless with "extra" words when revising your picture book text; they are words that add nothing to the story.

Often the writing at the beginning of a manuscript is weaker than what follows. This is where you can be particularly ruthless in weeding out chunks of text, especially if you are a writer who tends to discover your story as you write. Allow yourself those early ramblings and settlings-in, by all means, if you find it helps you to get into the story. But remember that a lot of that writing can often be cut. Don't feel so attached to your words that you wind up leaving them on the page at the expense of your story.

As noted earlier, eliminating words that will be "told" in the book's pictures is another place to begin. For example, you need not write, "The house was white with green shutters and a red door", if readers will see that in the illustrations.

It might help, too, to imagine you're paying for each word you use. Suddenly you see words, phrases, sentences, even paragraphs, that can be completely eliminated without sacrificing anything of importance to your story.

For example, does "One day Timothy's friend said.." say *significantly* less to readers than "One day Timothy went to his friend Michael's house and Michael said . . ."? It depends on whether readers *need to know* that Timothy went to his friend's house and/or that his friend's name was Michael.

The point of keeping your language simple and spare is not because children cannot understand it any other way, but because your writing will be more forceful if you do. One example of a powerful, haunting story, simply and sparely told, is Dyan Sheldon's *The Whales' Song*, about a patient girl for whom the whales finally sing one night.

If you have made use of repetition because a lot of best-selling picture books seem to do that, have you done it effectively?

Bonnie McSmithers you're driving me dithers, and blithery blathery out of my mind! What am I going to do with you?

from *Bonnie McSmithers* by Sue Ann Alderson

Jillian Jillian Jillian Jiggs it looks like your room has been lived in by pigs! Later I promise. As soon as I'm through. I'll clean up my room. I promise. I do.

from Jillian Jiggs by Phoebe Gilman

Are you my mother? he said to the —. . . . The — was not his mother. So the baby bird went on.

from Are You My Mother? by P.D. Eastman

Clang-clang, rattle-bing-bang Gonna make my noise all day. Clang-clang, rattle-bing-bang Gonna make my noise all day.

from Mortimer by Robert Munsch

There are lots of books in which the repetition of key phrases is part (sometimes a large part) of their appeal for children. However, if the repetition is to be effective, it should be related to the central idea of your story, as the examples above are, not just there for the sake of repeating random phrases or words.

Have you told your story in rhymed verse?

If yes, ask yourself why. If you are convinced you have a good reason for telling a story this way, go ahead. There was certainly no other way for Janet and Allan Ahlberg to do *Each Peach Pear Plum*, their delightful hide-and-seek book featuring nursery rhyme characters. But keep in mind that rhyme is not easy to write. It's just easy to write badly.

Publishers have received so much rhymed verse that is badly done that it has gained a bad reputation in the industry, to the point that many publishers say, "Don't send us rhymed verse." It's not because rhymed verse is inherently bad, but because the badly done stuff has created such a resistance to it you may be presenting yourself with a needless obstacle if you insist on writing in rhyme a story that does not on its own insist on being told that way.

But suppose your story is crying out to be told as rhymed verse, as must have been the case in the story of the cat who created such havoc when he came to entertain one rainy day — *The Cat In The Hat* by Dr. Seuss — and the story of the girl with a lion for a watchdog — *Lizzy's Lion* by Dennis Lee. How will you know if your rhyme is badly written or not?

If the making of rhymes seems to be dictating the story, as in "Geez, I need a word here to rhyme with truck — ah! luck!" or "Hmm, if I just move this adjective to the end of line three, it will rhyme with line one", then beware. And if, as you read your story aloud, the rhythm and the rhyming feel forced, or in any way distract from the story, consider it badly done.

In any area, and poetry is no exception, read what's current to help you decide if what you're doing fits in. (*Til All the Stars Have Fallen*, an anthology of traditional and contemporary poems selected by David Booth, would be an excellent place to start.) If it doesn't, be sure you know why before you send it off to a publisher or inflict it on your children.

Have you written your story in a way that makes what happens in it matter to readers?

To make it matter to readers that a teddy bear named Corduroy should find a home, Don Freeman relied somewhat on his readers' own experiences of feeling unwanted, knowing that most children would understand that feeling in a general way. However, to make readers care that this *particular* character, Corduroy (after whom Freeman's book is named), should find a home, it was necessary to establish early in the story how important it was to Corduroy by providing the details of Corduroy's life in the department store, and the details of Corduroy's first encounter with Lisa, the girl who ultimately comes back to purchase him.

Generally speaking, things matter in a book when the reader is allowed to get involved. This may depend — and it holds no less true of a picture book than it does of a juvenile or adult novel — on whether the writer is *showing* readers the events of the story or *telling* readers about them. It is more effective in establishing reader identification to show the sweat beading on the brow, the lip trembling, the stomach knotting, the knuckles cracking, than to tell readers that your character was nervous. Showing allows readers to feel what the character is feeling.

The use of direct quotes vs indirect quotes might help to illustrate this point further. Which puts the reader in closer touch with the events of the story?

Jack heard the giant say some strange words, and then he said he would do something awful to Jack when he found him.

or

Fee fi fo fum, I smell the blood of an Englishman. Be he alive or be he dead I'll crush his bones to make my bread.

CHAPTER FOUR

Beginnings, middles, and endings

Does the beginning of your story grab the attention of your readers?

The opening words of many successful picture books tell readers what the book is about. If they also define the problem to be solved in the story, that tension, which will be sustained throughout the successful telling of the story, is created immediately.

Franklin could slide down a riverbank all by himself. He could count forwards and backwards. He could even zip zippers and button buttons. But Franklin was afraid of small dark places and that was a problem because . . . Franklin was a turtle. He was afraid of crawling into his small dark shell.

from *Franklin in the Dark* by Paulette Bourgeois

Amos was old and Amos was cold and Amos was tired of giving away all of his wool.

from *Amos's Sweater* by Janet Lunn

My mom doesn't understand about red.

from *Red Is Best* by Kathy Stinson

It sounds obvious to say that you must grab your readers' attention at the beginning of your story. But reread your beginning again. Have you done it? Or have you meandered around events that prepared you, the writer, to get on with telling the story, but have little bearing on what your story is actually about?

Or have you begun with a cliché like "Once upon a time. . ." or "Long ago and far away. . ."? Of course, many fine books begin with these lines, but do beware that these openers are clichés. Use them only if they genuinely suit the story you are telling, if you are trying to distance readers immediately from the real and current world in which they are living.

Does the middle of your book keep readers turning the pages till they get to the end?

Many picture books, whatever the original intention of the author, are not read from beginning to end. As parents introduce their children to books at increasingly early stages of their development (a practice I wholeheartedly support), the pages of books are often enjoyed randomly. In many books, such as Richard Scarry's *Best First Book Ever*, or my own *The Bare Naked Book*, there is not a story which requires a sequential reading of the pages for enjoyment. In the case of books like this, and concept books about things like shapes or opposites, it may be enough to ensure that there is lots on each page for readers, usually a very young child and parent or other caregiver, to explore together.

However, if your book is telling a story, it is important that there be not only lots to explore on each page in terms of action, ideas, or feelings, but also a reason for readers to turn to the next page, and the next.

There may be a seductive pattern in the telling of the story or a compelling build-up of events. In any case, the pacing must be such that your readers will be helpless, once captivated by your opening lines, to do anything but continue to the very end.

Does your story have a truly satisfying ending?

Picture book readers want a warm satisfied feeling when a story ends. How comforting it is in Maurice Sendak's *Where the Wild Things Are* when Max returns from his adventure to find supper not only waiting, but still hot.

Confront your readers with problems, frighten them if you will, but always, always ensure that equilibrium is restored by the end of your story. Not that every story must end "happily ever after", but resolve things as best you can on a positive note. Where it would be dishonest to hold out to a child of divorced parents hope for a reconciliation, it might be appropriate to conclude with the reassurance that both her parents still love her.

A child can take seeing his own ups and downs reflected in a book, as long as it ends on an up note. Even Alexander, at the end of a day in which nothing seems to go right, seems able to understand, in Judith Viorst's *Alexander and the Terrible, Horrible, No Good, Very Bad Day*, that "some days are like that. Even in Australia."

Since children so often feel oppressed as members of society — everyone seems to have more privileges and authority than they have — a story is likely to leave a feeling of satisfaction if the main child character in it finishes in a position of strength. Let your character have the last word, as the giant's toe does in Brock Cole's book called *The Giant's Toe*. The toe in the story is depicted in the illustrations as a small naked child who outsmarts the giant (who, it turns out, is "Jack's giant", the one at the top of the beanstalk), foibles his attempts to do away with him, and makes him see that they're just going to have to get along together.

Be sure that the ending is tied tightly to what the story is about. If the beginning of the story is good, it might help suggest an ending. (And vice versa.)

CHAPTER FIVE

Characters

Have you avoided the use of glaring stereotypes?

Everyone is familiar with tales in which there is an obvious "good guy" and an obvious "bad guy". With considerable predictability, the "good guy" in such tales is beautiful or handsome, the "bad guy" is ugly. Of course, beauty and goodness, ugliness and evil, do not necessarily go hand in hand, but this kind of stereotyping is so common that it is understandable if readers come away from such tales with the impression that they do.

Literature should broaden a child's experience of the world, not confine it to narrow definitions. This is not to say that traditional tales which contain such stereotypical portrayals ought to be discarded, never to be read again. Rather, creators of new tales ought to be aware of the characteristics they bestow upon the characters in their work so that such glaring use of stereotypes can be avoided. Clearly it is worthwhile for young readers to encounter the occasional nasty beautiful person in a story, as well as an ugly person capable of performing kind or valuable acts.

What a marvelous twist on the helpless princess stereotype when Elizabeth turns on Ronald in Robert Munsch's *The Paper Bag Princess*, refusing to marry him because he is more interested in her appearance than in her bravery and strength.

Many people have grown up with attitudes to various ethnic or racial groups that are without foundation in fact. How easily such attitudes can creep into one's writing. Why is it that the brainy kid in your story is Oriental, for example, or that the good-natured, slow-moving one is black?

Examine your characters closely. You do not want to perpetuate myths in your writing or to offend readers thoughtlessly. Sex and race might be the most obvious areas to be aware of, but stereotypes to do with the aged, the disabled, and countless other segments of humanity are being challenged too. Stereotypes have a way of becoming so ingrained that writers need to take special care to avoid them, so that they are not inadvertantly passed on to another generation of readers.

How old are the characters in your story?

Many writers, particularly novice writers, worry too much about this and so begin their stories with such uninspired statements as "Jimmy was six years old." Perhaps this is because they've heard generalizations like "Five-year-olds only want to read about kids a bit older than they are."

But there are many successful books for children which aren't about children at all. One recent example is Janet Lunn's *Duck Cakes for Sale*, about a woman who goes into business selling duck cakes made with the overabundance of eggs her ducks are laying.

While the actual age of your characters may not be of great importance, how you establish the age of your characters is.

Rarely is it effective to tell readers the age of a character in the first sentence, nor should it be necessary. If there are enough clues in the story (and bear in mind that the illustrations will provide visual clues too), then readers will be able to deduce the age of the character without being told. Is she interested in attending baseball games, is he old enough to go downtown by himself, does her best friend have a paper route, does he confide in his teddy bear? Clues like these can help establish for your readers the age of the character you are writing about.

Don't try to create a character with a generic age to appeal to kids of all ages. Make characters "real" and no one, including you, will need to be preoccupied with their ages. They'll appeal to readers because, as "real" characters, you have made them live.

Do the adults in your story, if there are any, threaten to take it over?

If the main character in your story is an adult, then certainly the story will be his or hers. However, there are many manuscripts written about children that the authors allow to be stolen from the children by a well-meaning adult in the story. Either the adult steps in as the authority on something that the children might learn more joyfully through their own discovery, or the adult steps in to solve a problem that has grown too large for the poor incompetent children at the end of their resources. In both of these instances the story no longer belongs to the children in it and therefore does not belong to its child readers either.

The problem is not that adults aren't more knowledgable about some subjects than kids, or that they aren't sometimes needed to help solve problems. But most kids do not want to be reminded in books of their dependence on adults. They need to feel a sense of their power, in their lives and, at the very least, in their literature.

CHAPTER SIX

Handling elements of fantasy, mystery, humour, history, and fairy tales

Have you properly prepared readers for any fantastic elements that appear in your story?

Fantastic elements are those elements in a story that are not realistic.

If, for example, a horse suddenly speaks to a little girl, or if the main character is suddenly transported to another world, the reader must be prepared in some way, seduced as it were into believing, at least for the duration of your story, that such things can happen.

If something happens in your story that immediately makes the reader say, "I don't believe that", it means the reader has lost trust in you as a storyteller, and the rest of your story suffers, no matter how convincingly you continue from that point. This is true of all writing, but the danger is even greater in fantasy writing.

To find out how to seduce your readers into believing the unbelievable, read fantasy that works, at all reading levels, to see how other writers succeed at it.

Read Maurice Sendak's *Where the Wild Things Are*, in which Max travels from his room, where he's sent for being mischievous (a "wild thing", his mother calls him), to a land where he's the ruler of all kinds of fantastic "wild things". Read Tim Wynne-Jones's *Zoom at Sea* and *Zoom Away*, in which a cat embarks on marvelous adventures with the help of his mysterious friend, Maria. Read Marie-Louise Gay's *Rainy Day Magic* and her *Moonbeam on a Cat's Ear*, in which the characters try to steal the moon from the sky. Read Chris Van Allsburg's *Jumanji*, in which the world of a board game comes ominously to life for the children playing it. Read Margaret Mahy's *The Boy with Two Shadows*, in which a boy is entrusted with the care of a witch's troublesome shadow.

How do these writers get you caught up in believing such things when you know deep down that they couldn't possibly happen?

Or could they?

Do the animals in your story behave believably? In other words, do they behave like animals?

If the characters in your stories are animals, ask yourself why, especially if they are talking animals. Many publishers for a long time refused to look at manuscripts containing talking animals, not simply because animals don't talk, but because they had seen thousands of manuscripts about talking animals that were badly done. The talking animals might have been pointless, or worse yet, cute.

But there are times when having an animal for your main character can make a story better than having a human main character, even if it is a human situation the animal finds itself in. Who better, for example, to suffer from a fear of the dark, and to provide some welcome distance between the afraid-of-the-dark reader and the afraid-of-the-dark character, than a turtle who is so afraid that he can't even go into his own shell? Paulette Bourgeois clearly had that figured out when she wrote *Franklin in the Dark*.

Although animals don't talk, children generally are able to suspend their disbelief when the animals in their books talk to each other, maybe because it is easy enough to believe that there might be an "animal language" which the writer has translated so that the reader can understand.

If a friendship develops between human character(s) and animal character(s), how you deal with this relationship is important. You will be most successful if you let the people behave as people and the animals as animals.

For example, people and animals don't communicate in the same way. A young girl might wave goodbye to a squirrel. But if the squirrel waves back, this is likely to jar the reader and spoil the intended impact of the moment. A reader is much more likely to accept from the squirrel a flick of the tail before running off into the trees after the girl waves.

Since anthropomorphized animals are so easy to render badly, it is worth having a look at some that have been handled well: Amos in *Amos's Sweater* by Janet Lunn, Petunia in the books about her by Roger Duvoisin, Peter in *The Tale of Peter Rabbit* by Beatrix Potter, Harry in the books about him by Gene Zion, Ping in *The Story About Ping* by Marjorie Flack.

One of the best stories ever about anthropomorphized animals, and it is so wonderful that I will mention it here even though it is not a picture book, is E.B. White's *Charlotte's Web*, about a spider, a pig, and an assortment of other barnyard animals. It is worth noting that the animals in this story speak only to each other, not to Fern or the other human characters in the story.

Is there something in your story to create the kind of tension that gives a sense of purpose to your readers?

If asked why you could not put down a particular book, you would probably refer to suspenseful elements in the story. Although a picture book will be read literally in one sitting, it needs that element of suspense too, if the reader is to feel compelled to finish it.

If your story is based on a mystery — who stole the cooling cookies from the windowsill, or where did Lucy lose her beloved blanket? — then clearly your readers' interest in solving this mystery will carry them through the story. Or if the mystery is not revealed until very late in the story, readers will find themselves committed to rereading it, perhaps again and again, in an effort to solve the mystery, as is the case with Graeme Base's *The Eleventh Hour*.

But even stories that are not mysteries are much helped if they contain suspense similar to that which propels a mystery forward.

Sometimes a writer will produce a picture book manuscript that has a very sensuous feel to it, one that recreates a time and place that was special to the author as a child, one rich in language and imagery. While this kind of background will enhance a story, there needs to be something creating a tension that will compel your readers to read through to the end. Joan Reimer Goman's *Rebecca's Nancy*, in which the day-to-day routines of life in a Mennonite community play a large part, is made a much more compelling read because the main character has lost her much-loved doll.

For a picture book audience the suspense needn't be of the nail-biting cliff-hanger variety, but there should be a problem to be solved, or a question the reader wants answered before closing the book. In Gene Zion's *Harry the Dirty Dog*, will Harry be able to convince his owners that he's him after he's run away from home and come back unrecognizable? In Robert Munsch's *Mortimer*, is there anyone who can make Mortimer go to sleep? In Bernard Waber's *Ira Sleeps Over*, will Ira take his teddy bear when he goes to sleep over at Reggie's house? Will Reggie laugh if he does? In Virginia Lee Burton's *Mike Mulligan and the Steam Shovel* will Mike Mulligan and Mary Anne be able to dig the cellar for the new town hall in just one day, in spite of everyone's conviction that they're too old-fashioned?

Is your book funny? Yes? Good. Kids like funny books, right?

Lots of people will observe their own children, see them doing something that strikes them as funny, and try writing a story about it. But watch that humour. Is it enjoyed at someone's expense? Who thinks it's funny, or cute, when your toddler gets his pants on backwards, or his shoes on the wrong feet, for example? Probably not your toddler. If you are describing one of your children's experiences, try describing it through their eyes. How would *they* describe these experiences?

There may be humour in some of the things you write about, but if the humour is at the expense of a three-year-old child, it may not be enjoyed by the three-year-old reader as much as it is enjoyed by a parent or an older sibling.

In other words, be sure that the ideas, concerns, and observations of the characters in your book are appropriate to the ages of the children you hope will read it. If humour is slanted too much towards the adult audience, then you have not written a picture book for toddlers.

Sometimes there is humour in a story that is appreciated more by the adults reading it than by the children listening to it or reading it for themselves. That's okay, again as long as the laughs are not at the expense of the children, and as long as there is at least as much enjoyment in the story for the children as for the adults.

Witness John Bianchi's *Swine Snafu*. While there are certain lifestyle references in the story that only the adults reading it with their children are likely to appreciate, both adults and children can laugh at what happens when the Pigs' and the Boars' offspring, born on the same day at the same hospital, seem somehow to have got mixed up.

Similarly, in Catharine O'Neill's *Mrs. Dunphy's Dog*, both children and adults will laugh at the dog's varied reactions to the literature he reads, but adults will be able to appreciate the humour in a way that the kids enjoying the story probably won't, since they likely won't have read the books mentioned in the text themselves. Although kids might not fully understand the humour, at no point does Catharine O'Neill make kids feel excluded from the humour, or the butt of it.

Once you are sure that the humour in your story is something your intended readers would appreciate, consider whether it will stand up to the repeated readings a successful picture book must endure. If the whole story revolves around a sort of joke, then it may be funny, but only the first time it's read. For a picture book that "works", that's not enough.

While there are kinds of humour that get bigger laughs, the gentle kind in a story like Robert McCloskey's *Blueberries for Sal*, in which two sets of mothers and their offspring cross paths when on an outing in search of blueberries, keeps both adults and children returning to a book again and again.

Is there a jukebox in your log cabin?

It is possible to effectively and intentionally combine aspects of life from two different periods of history, as Phoebe Gilman did in *The Balloon Tree* when she brought balloons into a medieval setting. But anachronisms that are the result of sloppy research are inexcusable evidence of your lack of respect for your story and your readers.

Details help to create the world you want your readers to experience, whatever the story you are telling. In telling stories that take place in the past, whether it's ancient Greece or the time when your parents were children, such attention is even more crucial, on the part of both author and illustrator. The need for accuracy in historical detail is no less important for a picture book story, such as Monica Hughes's *Little Fingerling*, than for a work of historical fiction for adults.

If your story is a retelling of a folktale or legend, how have you made it your own?

If you are planning to inflict yet another version of any of the traditional folktales on readers, because you think retelling a story that's already been written might be easier than cooking up a whole new story of your own — think again.

The only reason to consider retelling legends or folktales from the body of existing literature is because you have something new to say about them or through them. Perhaps you would like to extend the role and/or circumstances of a minor character from a story, as Brock Cole did in *The Giant's Toe*. Perhaps you would like to show that the truths in an old story hold true in the modern world, as Fiona French did in her retelling of *Snow White*, set in the jazz age of New York. Or perhaps you feel there are new truths to be uncovered in a story, as did Jon Scieszka in his

The True Story of the Three Little Pigs, told from the point of view of the wolf. Or perhaps like Jean Little and Maggie de Vries you feel you can provide an entirely new twist on an old classic, not in the way they did it in *Once Upon a Golden Apple*, but in a way that is distinctly your own.

Celia Lottridge, author of the successful retelling of a Bantu legend, *The Name of the Tree*, has cautioned writers that just changing the setting of a story, or a character, without looking at what is important about that story will probably result in a thin version of it. A writer attempting a retelling, she underlines, must look at what is at the heart of the story, for the writer personally, because that is what will give the story depth in its retelling.

CHAPTER SEVEN

So you think your book is ready for readers?

Will a child learn something reading your book?

Of course, because you were paying attention in Chapter 1 of this book, you did not sit down to write your story because you had a moral lesson you wanted to teach children.

But remember the child in *Red Is Best*, who does not get frost bite after wearing mitts with holes in them, thereby learning that she ought to listen to Mom? Instead, because she wears the mitts of her choice, for her own reasons, she learns that she has control over some things in a world where she is essentially powerless. The author did not have that in mind when she wrote her book. She just recognized the universal nature of the adult/toddler power struggle, and the humour in it too, when she argued with her daughter one day over which stockings she ought to wear.

Watch for messages in your manuscript that you didn't think you put there. Would you want to write a book that suggests that it's not nice to be angry and that people will only like you if you don't express your anger? Or that because you are a girl you are more likely to bake cookies for the astronauts than to be an astronaut yourself? Or that parents only love their children when they're good? Not likely, but messages are often unintentional. And that's okay, as long as what children might "learn" from your book is something you'd want them to learn.

You wrote a story for the kids in your class or your own kids at home, and they liked it so much that you think you might send it to a publisher. Should you?

It depends.

Maybe you have written a story about a subject you know is popular in books for children. A child badly wants a pet that for various reasons a parent objects to. A child learns to deal with the death of a much loved grandparent. If you have written about such a subject, what makes your treatment of that subject different from what's been done before?

There are stories which come along that must be published, of course, regardless of how many exist on a similar subject. And yours may be one of them.

There are, for example, countless Christmas stories. And yet there was still room for Chris Van Allsburg's *The Polar Express*, in which a boy travels by train to the North Pole, chooses as his gift a bell from a reindeer's harness, loses it on the way home, and then finds it under the tree on Christmas morning. The language is rich, and just when you think the story has finished happily, there is another surprise for readers to enjoy. There was no way the publishers at Houghton Mifflin could read that manuscript and say, "Ho hum, another Christmas story."

Similarly, Anthony Browne's *Changes*, and *Daniel's Dog* by Jo Ellen Bogart, deal with the subject of a new baby sibling in a fresh and imaginative way.

Maybe you have written about a subject you have never seen dealt with in a book for children before. This may be cause for excitement. But you might ask yourself before you get too overwhelmed, if you are really the first person to think of writing on this subject, or is there another reason why there are no books instructing children as to the proper way to make a bed?

If the idea or subject of your book is one which publishers have been waiting to see, or have been hoping to see developed, they may be more open to your manuscript than if it feels like one they have seen many times before. Even if your writing is not superb, a publisher may be more willing to spend some time to help you develop your idea or subject if your book might fill a gap they are anxious to fill.

Finally, in considering whether to submit a story to a publisher with the implied hope that it be made available to many, many children, you might consider Bruno Bettelheim's words from *The Uses of Enchantment*:

> For a story truly to hold the child's attention, it must entertain him and arouse his curiosity. But to enrich his life, it must stimulate his imagination; help him to develop his intellect and to clarify his emotions; be attuned to his anxieties and aspirations; give full recognition to his difficulties, while at the same time suggesting

solutions to the problems which perturb him. In short, it must at one and the same time relate to all aspects of his personality — and this without ever belittling but, on the contrary, giving full credence to the seriousness of the child's predicaments, while simultaneously promoting confidence in himself and in his future.

That's a tall order. How does your story measure up?

CHAPTER EIGHT

Dealing with publishers

Are you absolutely sure that your manuscript has something so special to offer that a publisher will be absolutely unable to resist it? Even when you put it in the middle of the pile of 200 or so manuscripts that arrived during the same month that yours did?

If you're not sure, then don't waste your time and money sending it off. Yet. While it's true that you won't get a story published if you don't submit it, there is little chance that a manuscript you yourself have little confidence in is going to be in the small percentage of manuscripts that make their way from the massive "slush pile" to publication.

Have another go at it, then see what you think.

Or put it away for a while. Even the most well-established writers have manuscripts in their files that are not ready for submission. Your manuscript might stay in the drawer forever, or an idea that would transform it might come to you when you're waiting for the bus one day, or while you're running the water for a bath.

Or, before exposing it to the scrutiny of a harried publisher, seek out another opinion of your work — besides the enthusiastic but perhaps ill-informed and/or biased opinion your mother may have offered you.

Taking a writing course or taking part in a writing workshop will provide you with more objective, better-informed feedback on your work.

If there is a writer-in-residence at your local library or university, take advantage of the services they are offering. Their professional evaluation of what you have written may help you decide whether to take the big step or not, or it may enable you to revise your previously rejected manuscript in such a way that it will attract a more favourable response, as was Bill MacLean's experience with *The Best Peanut Butter Sandwich In The World.*

Freelance editors are sometimes available to offer a professional critique of manuscripts too. Of course, there is a fee involved for this service. Bear in mind that even if the freelance editor thinks your manuscript is marvelous, it will have no direct bearing on your success in finding a publisher.

You are convinced you have written the great picture book text of all time. Where should you send it?

To obtain a list of publishers of children's books currently accepting unsolicited manuscripts, contact any of the following organizations, depending on where you live. (Sometimes they offer more than just information about publishers.)

The Canadian Children's Book Centre exists for the promotion of the reading and writing of children's books in Canada. You can visit the Centre in person, request information by phone at (416) 975-0010, or write The Canadian Children's Book Centre at 35 Spadina Road, Toronto, Ontario, M5R 2S9.

The Centre produces an inexpensive kit of information for people interested in writing for children and numerous other publications and resource materials, including a quarterly newsletter which is available at no charge.

The British counterpart to this organization is The Children's Book Foundation, at Book House, 45 East Hill, London, SW18 2QZ. Their phone number is 01-870-9055.

The American counterpart is The Children's Book Council, at 67 Irving Place, New York, NY, 10003. Their phone number is (212) 254-2666.

What should you say in your covering letter?

Tell the publisher why you are submitting your manuscript to them. If you don't know why, or if it's because they're seventh on the list and seven is your lucky number, then you need to do some more research about who is publishing what. It cannot be emphasized too often how important it is to familiarize yourself with potential publishers' books before submitting a manuscript.

As a courtesy, tell the publisher if you are submitting your manuscript to other publishers besides them. You need not tell them who the others are. However, if you accept an offer from one of the publishers, do notify the others that you have found a home for your manuscript. Any publisher will rightly resent taking the time to read something to which someone else has already obtained rights.

Tell the publisher anything you'd like about yourself that gives them a sense of who you are, possibly including why you are writing children's books.

Don't bother to tell them that you tested your story on the neighbourhood children, your own children, your grandchildren, your nieces and nephews, the children in your class — and they loved it. Publishers will not be impressed by this because they know that the pleasure you saw in the children's faces as they listened to your story most likely came from the honour they felt at being asked an opinion.

Whatever you tell them, be brief. A page is sufficient.

Remember to sign your letter.

Is there anything special you should do to ensure that your manuscript gets the attention it deserves?

Both your covering letter and your manuscript should be clearly typed. Proofread everything carefully. Publishers see a vast number of unsolicited manuscripts, and a sloppy presentation will count against you.

Although publishers are generally careful with the work submitted to them, manuscripts are occasionally lost. Never submit the only copy of a manuscript you have.

Be sure to include a stamped self-addressed envelope for the return of your manuscript too.

What do editors do?

Some novice writers believe that good texts go straight from their hands to their editors and on to the printers. The reality, however, is that virtually every manuscript, no matter how good, needs some editing. It may involve small changes like correction of spelling or punctuation errors, or larger ones. Sometimes a story may go through several exhaustive rewrites before an editor accepts it.

It's important not to take editorial criticism personally, even though, when you have put heart and soul into a story, it's not easy to see it criticized and pushed and pulled in different directions. If an editor has expressed interest in your work, they are already on your side — and the side of the story; listen to their comments and questions, give them time to sink in, and don't be tied to your original version unless you can offer yourself, as well as the editor, good reasons why it should stand as is. If, for instance, you have written a largely autobiographical story, don't refuse to change it "because it happened just the way I wrote it". An editor, who can be more objective than you in a case like this, may be able to see changes that will improve the story, even if they make it less like the events you have based it on.

The editorial process does not always run smoothly: you may strongly disagree with your editor at times. But the process is, like so much in the publishing of picture books, a collaborative one, resulting, in most cases, in a better book — for the writer, the editor, the illustrator, and the reader.

CHAPTER NINE

Illustration

Should your manuscript be illustrated before you submit it?

Anyone who is not a professional illustrator with the technical training needed for book illustration, as well as the artistic ability, should not come near your manuscript with a paintbrush or a piece of chalk. Not your brother, not your friend, not your talented aunt who would like to illustrate your book.

But what if your brother, your friend, or your aunt happens to be a professional illustrator with the technical training and artistic ability needed for book illustration? What then?

Whatever the case, an already-illustrated manuscript is in a tricky position when it arrives on an editor's desk. The illustrations may be wonderful. But even the most beautiful illustrations will not help to sell a manuscript that does not stand on its own. The publisher may decide to work with the illustrator of this beautiful work, on another project, but the illustrations will not have much, if any, influence on the acceptance of your manuscript.

Then again, the illustrations may be mediocre or amateurish, or they may just happen to be everything in illustration this particular publisher detests. While it is possible that the publisher will accept your story but not your friend's artwork, many publishers would rather just return the whole package than get involved in the potentially tricky situation of accepting only part of it.

If you do submit art, do not risk damage or loss by sending original copies: good colour photocopies, prints, or slides are perfectly adequate.

But what if you are a writer and illustrator and you want to illustrate the story yourself?

The same potential problems exist as do if someone else has illustrated your manuscript. However, at least if you are both writer and illustrator and the publisher wants to work with only one or the other, it is you who has found work in either case.

Of course, it is possible that a publisher will accept your work as an author *and* an illustrator. But at some point you need to do some soul-searching to determine how you feel about having your writing and your artwork separated. Would you be willing to have your manuscript illustrated by someone else if a publisher did not care for your artwork? Would you be willing to illustrate someone else's manuscript if a publisher did not want your story? These are questions you might well be faced with. If you know the answers now, you might want to include this information in your covering letter.

Since submitting text and illustration together is a fairly risky business, don't plan on submitting a fully illustrated text. Two or three pieces of finished work that demonstrate your technique and your ability to maintain a character likeness from various points of view and in different moods, along with some rough sketches, or perhaps a rough lay-out of the book, are sufficient. Remember to send copies, not originals.

What does good illustration do for a picture book text?

Usually the work of the writer comes first. But it is the work of the illustrator that will first capture the attention of the parent in the bookstore, or the child at the library.

As you continue to read lots of picture books, in bookstores and libraries and homes where there are children, you'll find yourself rereading old favourites and discovering new ones, undoubtedly noticing the illustrations, even if it is the texts that you are studying.

Sadly, there will be books you suspect have been written, not very well, as an excuse to showcase an artist's work. There will also be books in which the illustrations seem like mere decoration, or as if they're just there as a way of breaking up the text on the page.

But fortunately for the thousands of readers being introduced to the rich world of books, there will be books in which you will find things in the illustrations that are not in the text, and vice versa. The illustrations will contain a story additional to that which the writer wrote. Often there will be details which go unnoticed on the first reading, little gems to be discovered as the book is read and reread again and again, which it will be if both the text and the illustrations are strong.

The balance between good text and good illustration is like a marriage. Each partner contributes his or her particular qualities and they complement each other. One does not overshadow the other. The reader's recognition of the happy balance of good text and good illustration is not a conscious one. The words and the pictures just "feel right" together.

Study the picture books referred to in this book (listed in the bibliography at the back), and go out and discover your own new and old favourites, and you will see what I mean.

When a talented writer and a talented illustrator bring to a book the best they have to give, then you are likely to overhear them referring to the book as "our book", and this is as it should be.

"I'm a writer, not an illustrator. How will an illustrator for my work be chosen?"

Established publishers have knowledge of and access to a large number and a large variety of illustrators, artists they have worked with in the past and artists whose work they have on file. It is unnecessary, and usually inadvisable, to have someone illustrate your manuscript before submission. (See Chapter 8.) Once a publisher has accepted your manuscript, they will want to choose an artist whose style complements your text, an artist your text will "speak to", an artist they know is reliable, not to mention available.

If you are fortunate you will be consulted about the artists being considered as potential illustrators of your text. The final decision rests with the publisher, but it is the wise publisher who recognizes the importance of respecting the writer's opinion. If you are familiar with current book illustration, you may even want to suggest an artist or a style of art yourself. Don't be surprised or upset if the publisher does not follow through on your suggestion.

Sometimes a publisher will show a manuscript to two or three artists and ask them to submit a few rough sketches on spec, with the understanding that only one of these people will get the job. If this is the case you might ask to be involved in the evaluation of these submissions.

What if the illustrator doesn't see the story the way you do?

It is best not to get too firm an idea in your mind beforehand of what your book is going to look like. Leave yourself open to the infinite possibilities that an artist might bring to your text and chances are good that you will be pleasantly surprised.

If, however, the artist seems to be missing the whole essence of your work, or is doing work that totally repels you, it is worth discussing the matter with your publisher, calmly and rationally. To help keep the tone of your discussions professional, keep in mind that you, the publisher, and the illustrator are all after what is best for the book. There is no room for egos in this kind of discussion.

"Will I get to meet the illustrator?"

Whether there is an actual meeting of author and illustrator may be determined by geography as much as anything. It is possible that all communications between you and the publisher and/or the artist will happen by letter, telephone, fax, or courier, depending on where in the country (or world) you are all situated. This is less important than the publisher's philosophy regarding the relationship between author and illustrator.

Some publishers prefer to deal with the writer and the artist separately. But many publishers recognize the advantages of having the writer and the artist working in consultation with each other. Such an arrangement enables the writer and the artist to exchange ideas directly. It may be possible for a writer to say, "I was hoping such-and-such a detail might be included in one of the pictures," or for an artist to say, "Is it important that this building be such-and-so, because I think it would look great if it could be such-and-thus." While this might create the occasional conflict that a publisher would prefer not to have to deal with, what results from such a collaboration, as long as there is mutual respect for each other's work, is often a better book than if the two professionals were working in isolation, a book that author and illustrator — not to mention readers! — are immensely pleased with.

Groups and organizations

"How can I go about meeting other writers?"

Writing is a solitary occupation. At times the feedback and support of other writers is important.

Many communities have informal writers' groups which meet regularly to discuss current projects, to exchange information, and to provide each other with encouragement. If you are unable to locate such a group in your community, you might try establishing one yourself, perhaps by advertising your interest in doing so on the bulletin board at a public library or a bookstore.

A more structured arrangement is to be found in a writing class. Many community colleges, universities, and boards of education offer evening (and sometimes day) classes for people interested in writing. Some specialize in writing for children. Contact any organization offering courses in your area for more information.

Watch for children's literature conferences being held in your area too. The line-up of speakers at such conferences often makes it worthwhile to attend, even if you have to travel some distance to do so.

In Canada, if you live in the Toronto, Vancouver, or Halifax areas, you might want to attend CANSCAIP meetings. CANSCAIP is the Canadian Society for Children's Authors, Illustrators, and Performers. It consists of professional members, who have had work published and/or performed, and associate members, who either aspire to having their work published and/or performed or have an interest in the business of writing for children. If you do not live in an area where attending meetings is possible, you might still want to consider membership in CANSCAIP, in order to receive the quarterly newsletter which contains information of considerable interest to people writing for children. For more information about CANSCAIP contact: CANSCAIP, P.O. Box 280, Station L, Toronto, Ontario, M6E 4Z2.

For information about comparable groups in Britain, contact: The Children's Book Foundation, Book House, 45 East Hill, London, SW18 2QZ. In the United States contact: The Children's Book Council, 67 Irving Place, New York, NY, 10003.

Conclusion

A book like this runs the risk of sounding as if there is a set of rules, and if you follow the rules, then you will write a picture book that "works". But of course, there are no rules, no magic formulae. And for every "tip" in this book, suggesting what works or what doesn't, there are probably exceptions. If you know what they are, you are in a strong position as a writer. And it is because you are a reader.

As a reader, you know the special joys to be found between the covers of a book — the excitement, the comfort, the magic, the friends. As a reader interested in writing picture books, it is important to you that children, too, know the special joys you have discovered.

It is between the covers of picture books that children first learn that books are interesting and enjoyable places to be. It is there that a life-long relationship with books begins. If it is reading that we want kids to fall in love with when we present them with picture books, then it is crucial that the words in those books are the best words we can find.

Go find them. Go write them.

Bibliography

PICTURE BOOKS

Alexander and the Terrible, Horrible, No Good, Very Bad Day by Judith Viorst, illustrated by Ray Cruz. Macmillan, 1972.

The Amazing Apple Book by Paulette Bourgeois, illustrated by Linda Hendry. Kids Can Press, 1987.

The Amazing Egg Book by Margaret Griffin & Deborah Seed, illustrated by Linda Hendry. Kids Can Press, 1989.

Amos's Sweater by Janet Lunn, illustrated by Kim LaFave. Groundwood Books, 1988.

Are You My Mother? by P.D. Eastman. Random House, 1960.

The Balloon Tree by Phoebe Gilman. Scholastic, 1984.

The Bare Naked Book by Kathy Stinson, illustrated by Heather Collins. Annick Press, 1986.

The Best Peanut Butter Sandwich in the World by Bill MacLean, illustrated by Katherine Helmer. Black Moss Press, 1990.

Best First Book Ever by Richard Scarry. Random House, 1979.

Blueberries for Sal by Robert McCloskey. Viking Press, 1948, 1976.

Bonnie McSmithers by Sue Ann Alderson, illustrated by Fiona Garrick. Tree Frog Press, 1974.

The Boy with Two Shadows by Margaret Mahy, illustrated by Jenny Williams. Collins, 1989.

The Cat In The Hat by Dr. Seuss. Houghton Mifflin, 1957.

Changes by Anthony Browne. Walker Books, 1990.

Charlotte's Web by E.B. White, illustrated by Garth Williams. Harper & Row, 1952, 1980.

Corduroy by Don Freeman. Viking, 1968.

Daniel's Dog by Jo Ellen Bogart, illustrated by Janet Wilson. Scholastic, 1990.

Duck Cakes for Sale by Janet Lunn, illustrated by Kim LaFave. Groundwood Books, 1989.

Each Peach Pear Plum by Janet and Allan Ahlberg. Collins, 1978.

The Eleventh Hour: A Curious Mystery by Graeme Base. Stoddart, 1988.

Franklin in the Dark by Paulette Bourgeois, illustrated by Brenda Clark. Kids Can Press, 1986.

The Giant's Toe by Brock Cole. Farr, Straus & Giroux, 1986.

Harry the Dirty Dog by Gene Zion, illustrated by Margaret Bloy Graham. Harper & Row, 1956.

I Didn't Know That by Katherine Farris & the editors of *OWL* Magazine. Greey de Pencier, 1988.

Ira Sleeps Over by Bernard Waber. Houghton Mifflin, 1972.

Jillian Jiggs by Phoebe Gilman. Scholastic, 1985.

Jumanji by Chris Van Allsburg. Houghton Mifflin, 1981.

The Lightning Bolt by Michael Bedard, illustrated by Regolo Ricci. Oxford University Press, 1989.

Little Fingerling by Monica Hughes, illustrated by Brenda Clark. Kids Can Press, 1989.

Lizzy's Lion by Dennis Lee, illustrated by Marie-Louise Gay. Stoddart, 1984.

Maggie and Me by Ted Staunton. Kids Can Press, 1986.

The Man Whose Mother Was a Pirate by Margaret Mahy, illustrated by Margaret Chamberlain. Penguin, 1985.

Mike Mulligan and the Steam Shovel by Virginia Lee Burton. Houghton Mifflin, 1939, 1967.

Mom and Dad Don't Live Together Any More by Kathy Stinson, illustrated by Nancy Lou Reynolds. Annick Press, 1984.

Moonbeam on a Cat's Ear by Marie-Louise Gay. Stoddart, 1986.

Mortimer by Robert Munsch, illustrated by Michael Martchenko. Annick Press, 1985.

The Name of the Tree by Celia Lottridge, illustrated by Ian Wallace. Groundwood Books, 1989.

Once Upon a Golden Apple by Jean Little and Maggie de Vries, illustrated by Phoebe Gilman. Penguin, 1991.

Owl Moon by Jane Yolen, illustrated by John Schoenherr. Philomel, 1987.

The Paper Bag Princess by Robert Munsch, illustrated by Michael Martchenko. Annick Press, 1980.

Petunia by Roger Duvoisin. Knopf, 1950.

The Polar Express by Chris Van Allsburg. Houghton Mifflin, 1985.

Rainy Day Magic by Marie-Louise Gay. Stoddart, 1987.

Rebecca's Nancy by Joan Reimer Goman. Sand Hill Books, 1978.

Red Is Best by Kathy Stinson, illustrated by Robin Baird Lewis. Annick Press, 1982.

Snow White in New York by Fiona French. Oxford University Press, 1986.

The Story about Ping by Marjorie Flack, illustrated by Kurt Wiese. Viking, 1933.

The Swine Snafu by John Bianchi. Bungalo Books, 1988.

Taking Care of Crumley by Ted Staunton, illustrated by Tina Holdcroft. Kids Can Press, 1986.

The Tale of Peter Rabbit by Beatrix Potter. Frederick Warne & Co., 1902.

Thomas' Snowsuit by Robert Munsch, illustrated by Michael Martchenko. Annick Press, 1985.

Til All the Stars Have Fallen, poems selected by David Booth, illustrated by Kady MacDonald Denton. Kids Can Press, 1989.

The True Story of the 3 Little Pigs by A. Wolf as retold to Jon Scieszka, illustrated by Lane Smith. Viking, 1989.

The Whales' Song by Dyan Sheldon, illustrated by Gary Blythe. Hutchinson, 1990.

Where the Wild Things Are by Maurice Sendak. Harper & Row, 1963.

The Witch in the Cherry Tree by Margaret Mahy, illustrated by Jenny Williams. J.M. Dent & Sons Ltd., 1974.

Zoom at Sea/Zoom Away by Tim Wynne-Jones, illustrated by Ken Nutt. Groundwood Books, 1983/1985.

Horn Book Magazine (about books for children and young adults). The Horn Book, Inc., 14 Beacon Street, Boston, MA 02108.

Michele Landsberg's Guide to Children's Books (with a treasury of more than 350 great children's books). Penguin, 1986.

The New Republic of Childhood (A Critical Guide to Canadian Children's Literature in English) by Sheila Egoff and Judith Saltman. Oxford University Press, 1990.

Quill & Quire (Canada's Book News Monthly Since 1935). 35 Riviera Dr., Unit 17, Markham, Ontario, L3R 8N4.

The Uses of Enchantment: The Meaning and Importance of Fairy Tales by Bruno Bettelheim. Random House, 1975.

Words about Pictures: The Narrative Art of Children's Picture Books by Perry Nodelman. University of Georgia Press, 1988.

Writing with Pictures: How to Write and Illustrate Children's Books by Uri Shulevitz. Watson-Guptill Publications, 1985.

Written for Children by John Rowe Townsend. Penguin, 1965, 1974, 1987.

Publishing Acknowledgements

Every effort has been made to acknowledge all sources of material used in this book. The publisher would be grateful if any errors or omissions were pointed out, so that they may be corrected.

From *Amos's Sweater*. Text copyright © 1988 by Janet Lunn. Illustrations copyright © 1988 by Kim LaFave. A Groundwood Book/Douglas & McIntyre. Reprinted by permission.

From *Are You My Mother?* by P.D. Eastman. Copyright © 1960 by P.D. Eastman. Copyright renewed 1988 by Mary L. Eastman. Reprinted by permission of Random House, Inc.

From *Franklin in the Dark*. Text copyright © 1986 by Paulette Bourgeois. Reprinted by permission of Kids Can Press Ltd., Toronto, Canada.

From *Jillian Jiggs*. Copyright © 1985 by Phoebe Gilman. Reprinted by permission of Scholastic Canada Ltd.

From *Mortimer*. Text copyright © 1985 by Robert Munsch. Reprinted by permission of Annick Press, Toronto.